Jean

WHISPERS

WHISPERS

Prayers and poems
for personal growth

by Ross Kingham

Illustrated by Lyz Mole and
Deborah Durie Saines

JBCE

The Joint Board of Christian Education
Melbourne

Published by
THE JOINT BOARD OF CHRISTIAN EDUCATION
65 Oxford Street
Collingwood 3066
Australia

WHISPERS

National Library of Australia
Cataloguing-in-Publication entry.

Kingham, Ross, 1942–
Whispers

ISBN: 1 86407 037 4.

1. Meditation. 2. Christian poetry. 3. Christian life. I. Joint Board of Christian Education. II. Title.

248.4

First printed 1994.

Design by Robina Norton
Typeset by JBCE in Bodoni Book
Printed by Shortrun Books

JB94/3511

Contents

Preface 5

1. Fire-lit 9

2. Doves and Serpents 21

3. The Adoring 37

4. Remembrance 51

5. The Flowing 67

6. Passion 79

7. Coming 91

8. Secrets 107

9. Timing 143

Appendix I 155
   Index to Scripture Passages

Appendix II 156
   Barnabas Ministries Inc.

Preface

Contemplation, for some, signifies an aloofness from the world, or a luxuriating in monastic prayer rituals, or a passive acceptance of what is, or even an analgesic for the pain of modern life.

For me, it is the opposite: contemplation is such a drawing into the heart of God that the curtain is rent in two, inner idols and prejudices are exposed and burned, dogmas and reasoned faith statements are called into the severest questioning, all sources of ego-security are scrutinised and judged and the Creator and all created things are seen and heard with a brutal clarity.

Contemplation is wild joy and deep, deep wounding. It is both peace and bruising struggle. It is satisfaction and it is the most horrendous thirsting. It is Spirit moulding spirit.

These poems are products of such a human experience of God. They are more the gift of the Spirit – whispers of the Spirit – than the creation of the human spirit. They have evolved almost as if they have a mind of their own. This sense of poetry's independent wilfulness to exist is expressed well by A. A. Milne in his account of Piglet learning about poetry from Pooh:

> 'And that's the whole poem', he said. 'Do you like it, Piglet?'
>
> 'All except the shillings', said Piglet. 'I don't think they ought to be there'.
>
> 'They wanted to come in after the pounds', explained Pooh, 'so I let them. It is the best way to write poetry, letting things come'.
>
> 'Oh, I didn't know,' said Piglet.[1]

These fruits of contemplation are for the tasting. They have emerged from some of the most wonderful, and most blessed, but also some of the most agonising, of the experiences of my life. They were written in the snowfields, and in the heat of the far north of Australia and in various cities, aeroplanes, riverbanks, gardens and sundry other places. They reveal more of my own self than I would have preferred, but such self-revelation seems necessary for personal growth.

Lyz Mole has special and, I believe, inspired gifts as an illustrator. She has expressed some of her responses to the poetry in this volume. In a prayerful reflection on the poems, she is able to communicate through her drawings poetic insights which transcend the power of the written word. I am deeply grateful to Lyz for her willingness to submit to the process of letting these poems speak to her, and resonate in her spirit, to such an extent that she has been able to create the artwork in this book.

Deborah Durie Saines' artwork complements that of Lyz Mole. Her sketches highlight some of her responses to the images of the poetry, which for her 'touch all the senses and the heart'. The artwork is Deborah's response to the word-images of the poems – clear, simple lines capturing and exploring the varied themes. She uses drawing as a means of expressing her responses to the call of the Spirit.

What I have tried to convey in these poems is, to use David Malouf's expression, 'the close but inexpressible grandeur and terror of things, ordinary things which, if attended to in a certain way, glow with an extraordinary significance'.

Most of these poems emerged in my praying through stories in the scriptures. They were not written after prayers, as a reflection on the Bible reading and the praying. Rather, they came to me in the act of praying, in my encounter with God. And my prayer now is that these poems may be

...prophecy
Of a new heaven and earth,
A rumour of resurrection,[2]

and that the following pages will be for you fruit of the Spirit,
that will feed your spirit!

Ross Kingham

1   A. A. Milne, *The House at Pooh Corner*, Richard Clay (The Chaucer Press, Ltd),
    Bungay, Suffolk, UK., 1979, p. 29.

2   James McAuley, 'Credo', from *Collected Poems* 1936-70, (Collins/Angus &
    Robertson), 1971, p. 180. Reproduced by permission of HarperCollins Publishers.

FIRE-LIT

Fire mountain

Perhaps not enough of us
Have been to Horeb, mountain of fire,
Of burning bush,
Of lightning and thunder and smoke,
And meeting place.

We are called to different peaks,
Different mountains,
But the same igniting
In the depths
Of awesome hope
And wrestling trust,

Without which there is no going forward
Towards promise,
Only circling in yesterday's memories,
Quaint but not spirited,
Not relishing what is and what could be,
Lit
By that fire.

Exodus 3:1-12; Exodus 19

A so tender flame

THE Table offered us symbols,
Candles, bread, wine,
And spoke of, yes, tender flame.

Other fire destroys, distorts,
Annihilates its host;
But not this one.

This God burns in a bush
And all is enhanced in the burning,
Ringing with the Word of Fire.

And candlelit bread and wine
Depict the only victim
Of God's burning –
The Divine One dancing from the shadows
For all the barefoot ones
Who see –
On Golgotha the flames ascending
Tongues from the dark abyss
Rend his soul.

And new tongues,
Of Spirit fire
Caress
And, warming, bless
Love-filled children of the flame.

Exodus 3:1-6

11

Holy ground

Holy ground is safe.
Bare feet on deep pile carpet
Are massaged
Without tickling,
Relaxed,
At home.

Holy ground is hurtful,
Jabbing the soles.
Place to be vulnerable
Where stone and cut glass
Lodge.

Holy ground is slow
For the shoe-less.
It is so seen,
Each detail requiring consideration
Of the most delicate kind,
The journeyer picking the path
Gingerly,
Mindful of tender feet.
Choosing most carefully each foot-fall,
Marking each shape edge,
And hearing the birdcalls
And the wind in the trees.

Holy ground is lit bright
The flames leaping
And warming
And warning
Of a Presence
In the night
That merits
At least
An inward gasp of awe
For one disposed
To sensing
Fire.

Exodus 3:1-15

Two flames draw close

These my friends
Are being married today

And what can I say?

Two lives are being changed,
Two flames are drawing closer,
Two hearts
Merge
In the closest friendship,
A miracle melding
In the wild, sentimental,
Tough tenderness
Of marriage.

We, alongside,
Are touched in this merging.
We who have shared,
Some more,
Some less,
In their separate journeys

In their happiness,
And in their tears.

And now we
Meet
And greet
And know
We, too,
Have been changed,
Our lives enriched,
And we are grateful.

And the saints
In heaven

Dance
In sheer delight
For the love
Beyond price
We celebrate
Today.

Enjoy! Laugh!
Cry! Delight!
And grow in tenderness,
Together.

Lonely flame

Why the clutter?
The filling of every conceivable
Even the tiniest
Crevice
That could provide space
For the echoing of the Word,
The deepest shedding of light?

Why the starving of the flame
In dampened stained glass glow?

So many fine words
And sentiments.
Such symbolic movement and colour,
Even a tall candle lit
(A brief moment of dramatic effect
In a busy programme),
And the choir, puffing, in full flight.

Yes, it was a fine service of worship.
Everyone kept insisting it was so.

And, afterwards,
A friend
Blinking back tears
Breathed to me a prayer of agony
For which
I think
In worship
There had been no room.

How the Holy One must weep
At the stifling,
The One who would, if allowed,
Light candles

Sitting close,
Sharing the load,
Imparting joyful strength
To souls
Desiring flame.

Another fruit

Not all want this fruit.
Eve and Adam and I
Know one kind of desiring,
But hardly this.

A questing for another garden,
Other trees and vines and flowers
Of light and such rich colours
Eye squints, breath inhales
At such intricately ordered chaos,
Such full flavoured Spirit presence.

Now I am drenched in colours
Like a clown
Filled with laughter, splashing hues all over,
Lighting heart-candles,
Bearing a mystery,
Gleams of the rainbow
For a darkening world.

Galatians 5:22-23

God-flames

Those God-flames
Are everywhere
Burning.

And in my mind
I say 'Yes'
To being Spirit-lit,
Yet try
To leap
From the most intense heat
At the last moment,
Wanting controlled burning,
God's appearing
In the most attractive,
Most manageable of flames
Only.

But this baptism
Is mine,
Is ours.
This enveloping
Brilliantly burning
Colouring, warming
God
Dancing the earth,
Lighting the sky,
Freeing fickle hearts
For unquenchable fire making
In the waiting chill
Of world's evening.

Is mine,
Is ours.

Jesus: 'I came to bring fire to the earth, and how I wish it were already kindled! I have a baptism with which to be baptised, and what stress I am under until it is completed!' Luke 12:49, 50
(New Revised Standard Version)

19

Guttered candle

It's scary
In the melting.
Liquid wax pool
Moving from heat
To a quiet cooling
Lava-like
In unknown places;

Not knowing the beauty
Of the end place,
Slowly regaining
In a softer way
Colour
In the reforming,
Displaying for all with eyes to see
A muted, fluted magic,
Movement slowed for the seeing.

A flowing art form
Necessarily
Beyond the flame.

DOVES AND SERPENTS

Maverick

The maverick
Glows
With a self-confidence
That admits no need of strong friendships
To love,
Question,
Guide.

Mavericks love their own will
And find it sweet,
While claiming to hold
Truth
Fiercely.

In the name of Love,
They are obsessed with self-love,
And seek others to stroke and stoke
Their frightened, hollow egos.

Propelled by pain within,
They flail their way through life,
Sometimes with fleshly flair and style,
But, like fireworks in a crowded place,
Flame and die in spirit,
Mauling the Body
Grievously.

Mavericks move on
Seeking ever new sucking grounds
For the bloating
As a leech,
Leaving wounds
Desperate for a clotting agent
And hard, so hard to heal
Ever.

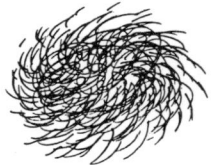

Banyan tree

All over, we whites have said,
In the name of Love,
We'll use your sweat
For sugar, flour, tobacco, and grog.
We'll sell your art
And copy it
For our own benefit – and yours, of course.
We'll allow your flair to help us
On the sportsfield.
We, the sporting nation,
Will make ourselves feel better
By finding fault in you.
We'll show you better ways,
Our religion, our culture, pure gospel
For the taking.

All over, we've planted our seed
Of plants with sweet fleshed fruit, and sour,
In your dark, mysterious, rich spirits.

We like the outcome, does us proud
At a quick glance
And think it has brought life to you.

Beware, the banyan tree.
Slowly it
Crushes its host.

Rape

He, only eight years old,
Was puzzled when the little girl's uncle
Urged him into the bathroom
And locked the door
On innocence.
How white those tiles,
Coldly, harshly clean.

He had thought the stranger
At the birthday party
Friendly.

Within minutes,
The rape was finished,
Could never be undone.

And the solemn pact made
The secret,
Never to be told.

Long years after,
He found a place
Where he could focus
That scene,
Hear again those party sounds,
Smell the useless bleach
And touch the horror
And the shame.

For something unmourned
Had died
On those white tiles,
Died in his heart
That sunny afternoon.

He wasn't sure he wanted manhood,
Though he only felt that way
Dimly.
Were men beasts,
Hurting and dirtying
With their grotesque bodies?
Was he destined also
To be crude and cruel and confounding?
Could he escape the imprint
In his mind
Of such a powerful brutishness?

Childhood was the happier
Because prolonged.
Growth was like autumn,
Feared for what it would herald.

Listening ears
And strong, caring hearts
Have borne so much,
Enabling the slow but sure
Miracle.
Necessary
But yet complete?

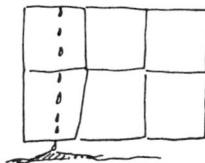

Legion

Do not subdue, Lord,
That which I fear most.
I love my many selves,
Each delighting to fire me
With inner agony,
The spirit-screaming of the night
Of a thousand voices
That echo in the tombs of my mind.

You know my powers scented
With such dark violence
That, at any moment, could
Unleash destruction,
Shatter with shards your image
In my friends,
And do.

Lord, have mercy,
Christ, have mercy,
Lord, have mercy.
Grant us your peace.
All of us.

Mark 5:1-20

Discernment

Knowing the spirits
Is fruit of a dangerous love,
Eve's choice
Become mine.

The serpent lurks in the garden
Urging good food,
A delight to the eyes,
Source of wisdom for my lips.

I devour after pausing briefly
Ravishing, gorging on Spirit food.
And am appalled at wisdom's power,
Ego-warped,
To divide and shame,
To name and blame
Wildly
Sin.

How gladly, yet fearing, I hear Another
Calling, caring, comforting
My torn spirit.
Heavenly seamstress,
Clothing, enfolding me
In softest fabrics.
Not now immune from serpent's fang
But strengthened strongly within
For the wounding and the walking.

Genesis 3

Serpent formed

Arnhem land secrets
Locked in patterns familiar
To tourists
Yes, that T-shirt design will look great on you!

Free-form design
Echoing ancient wisdom
Of sacred art.

The serpent shape
All over the marshy wetland world
Life-winding
River-threads of meaning
In a land
Rich in knowing.

For every flatness,
Symbol revealing
The darker light hidden
Fresh dawning.

Spirit seam

He was fortunate, really,
That the devil retired hurt.

After the savage storm had done its worst,
To now have oil on wounds
And the tenderest hands
Care for him,
And traumas of mind and spirit eased,
Nursed to a strength far stronger
By angels.

How the gales had whipped clothes, hair,
Flecks of superfluous desiring
Snapped clean away,
Every fibre of self pummelled,
Knotted parts shaken free,
Leaving that delicious calm
After the bracing,
Baptised again.

Now, after the rack,
More than ever
Trustful,
Having tapped a seam of courage
And a knowing
That could,
And would
Again,
Scatter darkness before him,
And before us,
Making way for Another.

Far better held, strengthened, loved,
For the nightmare tearing.

Matthew 4:1-11

Shadows

Shadows are light's closest friends.
The longest shadows bathe the land
Nearest the most splendid
Of light's comings –
Sunrise, and sunset.

Facing the shadows,
Those necessary spaces unlit
Gives a steely strength.
The contrasts require,
Demand,
Choice.

Without shadow, there is no freedom
To choose
Light or dark,
And the soul shrivels
As a salt-stung leech.

The most savage choices
Are demanded by those dark recesses
Within.
Shafts of darkness
Capturing a weakness here,
A strength there,
(Masquerading as if lit,
But perverted in ego's service),
Poisoning the spirit
As evil toadstools in a dark, cool forest
In the heart.

Stand still.
Face the shadows.
Grip them and twist them
And wrestle
The nightmare powers
And,
Turning again to light,
Gulp the freshness
Dancing in eyes and heart.

Matthew 6:23

One thing lacking

You lack
Because of a poverty
You have not yet embraced.
You would be more whole
If you would taste
Hunger.

You boast and brag a blight
Disguised as an asset
To impress yourself and others,
But a terrible weight in the soul.

You lack
Because you have, you hold
A glittering lie
Which now possesses you,
A cobra throttling your self,
Called 'My Spirituality'.

Name your fickle fancy
And it will, reluctantly, go.
But name it within,
Deep in the bear pit of the self
Or again the naming
Will draw attention to yourself,
The trap sprung.

Embrace true poverty of spirit
Not as a credential
For your fame,
But as for Me.

That's the trouble with greatness
That is true —
You can hardly recognise it
When you see it.

Luke 18:18-25

The lesser dream

There is a voice
From the darkness
That, seemingly spirited,
Mimics the voice of God,
Insisting that the lesser dream
Is enough;
That loving less
Than we are loved
Is more than could be expected;
That self-love
Is more necessary
Than any other.

Rather the flint-like grace
To cast deep
And aim high,
Shunning the middle way,

The mediocre, wearied,
Lack-lustre, faded reflection
Of a life
Profoundly risking
For the sake
Of others –
An immediate good
Corroding
What might have been,
Fiercely splendid.

Isaiah 50:7; Luke 9:51-62

The tightrope walker

Dazzling the crowds
With brilliant precision,
The tightrope walker fears
More than the dreadful spotlit tumble to sawdust
Crack and thump and trickle of blood,
That other nemesis:
The drawing, driving power
That would pulp his soul.

Strong adrenalin surge
Enables the act,
But leeches the spirit
Dreadfully

And the inner balancing act,
Always without a safety net,
More hazardous
Than the crowd would ever dream,
Imperils
And blanches
The most outrageous,
The most wonderful
And adorable and, even, pious
Of performers.

Adulation
And titillation
Of a fragile ego

Versus

Poverty of spirit,
Inly strong
Despite grease paint and drum roll,
And even the emptiness
Of the darkness
After the roaring crowds
Have dispersed
And every tiny speck of dust
Has settled.

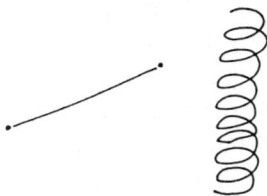

Matthew 5:3

Massah and Meribah

Surely to test God
Is not a crime?
To thirst and cry
In the unforgiving heat?

Rather, it is when need
Festers the soul
Not quite at peace
And infects others
In a whirlpool of bitterness
That saps the spirit
Of all
In the desert.

And the dry heat causes to dance
The jackals,
Beasts of the wilderness
That threaten the heart and blur the vision,
Feeding foul dreams of oases
Muddied with ingratitude,
Mirages of contention and contortion
And hypercriticism and disrespect,
Beckoning further towards,
Not refreshment,
But bleached bones.

What miracles lie in Horeb's rock!
Torrents of grace
Engulfing all petulance,
All presumption,
All pining
For the fulfilment of dreams
Of an easier path.

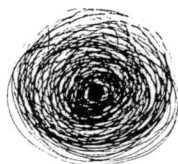

Exodus 17:1-7; James 3:14-18;
Hebrews 12:14-17

THE
ADORING

The adoring

There is a time for being singular,
Enjoying vertical slivers of grace
Alone.
We, who love community,
Need separateness too
For the adoring.

Protestants, thinking to be right
(The sign of true worship!)
Have argued long and hard
About the 'Real Presence':
Is that bread, that wine, now Christ?

These friends don't argue,
They adore.
For them, the one all-powerful drawing centre
Is not in music or preacher or any such thing.
For hours on end, day in, day out,
Their centre is God.
Their programme, Love.
They make their retreat with generosity of heart,
A gentle dropping of obsessions,
In silent devotion.
Not a whisper in the room of prayer,
Scarce a sideways glance,
Just carpet, stained glass windows and
The Blessed Sacrament.

Moved by the responding, sitting, kneeling, lying
In silent love-filled praise,
I, too, kneel and pray.

Silence

Sheer silence
Can be heard.

Beyond peacefulness
And harmony with creation
Is a boiling surf.
Inside.
Currents and eddies dredging my soul,
Voices within
Screaming,
Echoing off the walls of my mind.

And after the turmoil,
A Voice.

I am not alone
For that Voice,
Says,
'I know the turmoil
Within you.
I am in your struggle,
Feel your pain,
Visit your soul
Beside light colours
And dark shadows,
Gracing you with My presence,
Anointing your torn dreams
With the sweet sweet oil of my Spirit.'

1 Kings 19:11-13

Their fame, God's name

Some egos, like our cat, demand endless stroking
Beyond the word or smile
That often flows in gratitude.

A stroking that sickly pampers
The frightened spirit,
Drugs the pain,
Feeds the lust of a raging Nero,
The lust for self to be the adored centre –
The people-carers' trap.

These friends, though,
Are consumed with Another,
Walk the pathway each day
Under oaks and sycamores
In prayer.
As if they don't need a back-slapping,
Emotion-rending, fountain-of-wisdom
Spotlit part in the scheme of things.

Their thoughts, their loves,
Are sufficiently at peace
To walk softly.
Their fame, God's holy name
Adored in silence.

*Luke 5:15, 16 'His reputation
continued to grow, and large
crowds would gather to hear him
and to have their sicknesses cured,
but he would always go off to some
place where he could be alone and
pray'.* (Jerusalem Bible)

Mary

She had sobbed her love before.
Now, she cried her grief.

Her brother was dead.

Once, her tears had splashed Jesus' feet
As she poured out her aching soul to the
Source of life,
But now that Source was distant
And had failed her.

A double grief:
Grief of mourning,
And grief borne of a faith darkness.

Tears upon tears.

She went out hurriedly.

They thought she had fled to the tomb
To weep.
But instead, she ran to throw herself
Again at Jesus' feet
Wet them with her crying
And pour out her bruised, confused love to him,
Sorrow now flecked with anger,
Her love a fierce fire.

They went to the tomb,
But not to weep.
They laughed!
Then followed in freedom,
Heady, delicious freedom,
The One marked now for certain dying,
And more fiery love-tears yet.

John 11:1-54

Some sort of fisherman

It must be quite some sort
Of wandering prophet
Who'd call you from your failures,
Show you how to reach your star,
And then move your desires beyond
And away
To tread a new path.

The very heart of things
Had been cracked open
As the morning's sunlight flashed
In his hair, eyes, mouth,
Enough to throw you face down
On the salty sand,
Unequal to that gaze.

Strange, that for so long Simon had toiled,
Unlike the crowds.
Obsessed with the market, and hunger,
His bloodshot eyes for the moment
Beyond dreaming,
Not seeing the glow
On the beach.

And then it came,
As if a spell enveloped all four fishermen,
A net, cast by a carpenter,
Holding them gently,
Caught up, willingly, in his destiny.

Luke 5:1-11

Carpe Diem

The crowds were there that morning
– Wouldn't have missed it –
Listening, marvelling,
But the moment that could have claimed their
lives, their loves,
Was lost in seagulls' cries,
Put out, no doubt,
That pagan fishermen
Cursing their lot
But used to seeing significant things
Like a shift in the wind,
A ripple, the smallest turbulence,
Should see what had slipped them by.

Their listening ears,
Their striving to touch,
Forced him to turn to those
At the margins.
He used their boat,
Spoke their language,
Teased them a little, casting them a line
After his own futile fishing expedition
On that very beach
(They had much in common).

More than wise words to salt their living,
This one offered a reason which would brook
No rivals in the heart,
A love, a peace,
And the security of abandoning all
For the sake of a wandering preacher.

Luke 5:1-11

Bare feet

Peter thought nothing of striding out,
Arms held high in delight,
Bare feet splashing, dancing the wind-swept sea.

Bare feet
Are enough in that Presence
When with that other power.
Boots and dress shoes and slippers
Are needed for every other purpose,
To protect, impress, keep warm,
But not for this.

Skin mediates love.
Jesus' feet were anointed with perfume
And tears and kisses
And dust,
And stabbed with iron spike.

Skin feels burning bush heat,
The cold of a biting wind,
And the caresses of love.

It is not wave-washed feet that sink the spirit;
It is feeling the force of the night gale
Tearing face, hair,
The wind that howls from Golgotha's dark crest,
And letting the terror in.

They come to this place of prayer, mostly,
Unshod,
The shoe-rack full outside the room,
Reduced to common dependence,
Feeling the sustaining, sheltering one
Who has borne, is bearing,
The full weight
Of those winds
In the soul.

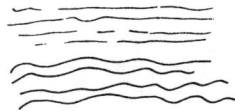

Matthew 14:22-33

Mosaic

In the fever they came.
Coloured spirits
Each streaming its own richness,
A fluid stained-glass window
In the mind
Beyond imagining.

Forming in the flowing a unique beauty
And yet in danger
Of the awful merging.
Watercolours splashed together
Before their time,
Every one muddied, diluted, drained,
A murky clone-scape
In the soul.

True beauty of spirit
Needs time to be
Of itself.
Nurtured enough,
Not engulfed,
Each its own brilliant artistry
From within itself.
Its own space, its own grace,
Laughing
In the so gentle touching.

Attentiveness

Rarely have I seen
Such fruitfulness.

Bursting from eucalyptus trees
Is such a display
Of blossom and nuts,
And from the sands
The banksia
Outpours
A multitude of flowers
Dripping in pollen,
The dark, mysterious branches
Adorned with pink lanterns,
And golden.

Why is it that I wander
Into other places,
Pursuing others things,
Anything at all?
— Not what is given
    In such intricate
    And wonderful
    Abundance?

What ache,
What longing,
Makes so hard the seeing,
The delighting
In all this beauty,
Borne of your so generous Spirit?

To the unknown God

Don't look for God with your eyes,
You probably won't see the One
Who gave you sight.

Look for God sensingly in bread,
In wine,
Slivers of light in common things,
The parabolic
That surround, indwell
Day by day.

Look for God roguishly, outlandishly,
Not always trying to see as others see.
Try gale-force wind and earthquake and fire
And the gentlest whisper
Of a summer breeze
Rustling the poplars.

Seek to sense the One
Who is not a trapped particle
Of creation
To be located, fixed, enshrined, harnessed;
But rather is behind
And through,
From which all comes,
To which all goes,
Without which all would dissolve.

Whom to know is freedom
Even in unknowingness.

Acts 17:23; 1 Kings 19:11,12

A free spirit

I have just completed
In clay
A prayer,
A dream of what might be,
A statement,
A cry
Now sitting candle-lit.

Lord, enlighten
My desiring
For you
And for your ways,
And kindle within me
The dreaming power
That is your gift,
My,
I pray, my
Choice.

Luke 10:39, 41, 42

REMEMBRANCE

Bread

Full slices
Simple, substantial
In fire flicker glow on a cold night
With butter.
Not like fairy floss or cream puffs
(All promise, but in the end
palate-cheating ruses).
Fresh, hot, yeast-breathed
Homely friend.
Communion evoker and sustainer for young
and old alike.

Bread is.
Other foods seem options only,
Full flavoured, maybe,
But not what is.

An endless array of loaves invite the hungry
Colours, breezes, stillness of rainforest,
Sunsets, wafers of music.
Tears from deep within
Are bread.
Some thoughts,
An occasional glancing touch
Or close embrace
Inflaming the soul.
Rare, chosen words are bread, too,
Rich full presence,
Everywhere showering amber crumbs
When steel slashed
By razor-sharp knives.

But fuller feast again,
The Word, broken into so many, many morsels
Strong food: Spirit feeding spirit
In that deepest union.
The eternal I am
In my, my mouth.
In our, our mouths.

Freshly yeasting with joy
The Body
And for such wild sweetness,
Such love-sharing, its breaking.
Always for the breaking.

John 6:32

Dream shadow

The fire
Once strong burning in those eyes
Was gone.
Ash grey residue only
Lined the sockets
Flecked with veins of soreness,
Red pock marks of pain long stifled.

Tears repressed, unbidden,
Moisten those ashes
So rarely
At the sound of a far distant echo
In the memory
Smudging, not cleansing, the heart.

The years of mid-life had bathed
Those tired eyes with a septic lotion
Acid burning,
Colour draining,
Dulling the last, piercing glint
Of wistful trust.

Memories, tarnished, warped,
Wafted and danced in the haunting shadows
More flimsy than air,
Evading true retina touch
Like elusive ghosts,
Beyond true embrace.

Can the seeing, the hoping, the fire
Not return, in far fuller measure?
The dancing reel and race?
The dream more powerful yet?

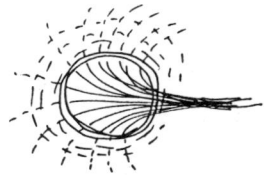

Old Man Rock

Nungalinya*
Ever renewing, enriching memories
Of root, rock treasure.

Stained in spirit strong sweat, tears,
feasting, paint, fear.
Cold throbbing with dance, music, laughter,
bull-roarer, didgeridoo.
Stories of dreamtime, deep-written in your
ancient heart,
Stone tablets uncleft,
Mosaic law of another tongue.

Witness of generations' secrets
Darkstained lichen host
Slow life-bearing still
Of visions
Honey-in-the-rock,
Water gushing succour
As torn from rib-cage,
Power of that other Rock
Embracing.

*'Nungalinya' is an Australian Aboriginal word for 'Old Man Rock'. A huge ancient rock stands outside Nungalinya College, Darwin, Australia. This college is the Combined Churches Training and Research Centre for Aboriginal Christian leaders of the Anglican Church, the Catholic Church and the Uniting Church in Australia.

The photograph

Yearning to retain images
Beyond surface retina gleanings,
She said in the early morning light
To her tourist companion
'Smile!'

Memories flooded her
Around and around
Fuelled by full matt colour
Post-card snap
Sweetly oscillating from
Fixed print
To that bright moment
Over and over in the mind,
Lingering matured wine flavour
Not quite forgotten.

And beyond the print
The shadow.
Strange innuendos in the ghostly negative
Glimpsing from inside another realm
Where light and dark seem contrary,
Hinting at that other
Which, yes, was there that morning,
Beyond camera-poise,
True full-spirited depth.

Beauty, fresh and clean.
Pain stab, jagged,
Searing imagination.
Words of peace whispered long ago,
Bus tickets in hand,
In that other place.
Sights, sounds, tastes,
Fragrances
Born afresh,
In mind-heart gasp.

Two for the price of one
Plus free film
Special offer.

Taste of resurrection
Newly flesh-framed.

Business card

I'd worked hard for those qualifications,
Listed for all to see
On Paper.

She asked my name, where I came from.
I had no skin colour. But I did have a card!
'See – my name, and here, the logo...'

Her eyes saw one thing –
'All those letters', she said.
'Look at them.'

I looked.

The conversation meandered on,
That look unforgotten.

My riches exposed at a glance by hers, who
Had lived in infancy in the back of a truck
And last year was refused accommodation
In a 'white' town
('We don't want you blacks here', they said)
And when she first went to church,
'Niggers are all pagans', said the preacher.

One look.

Spirit friend

She seemed so grateful
When I thanked her.

Not dismissive, embarrassed,
As I might have been.
But grateful
To the core
Of her spirit.

So thankful
I wince to think of it.

So joyful she was,
So at peace
In the naming and the owning
Of her giving.

I have seen that look before,
My sisters,
My brothers,
My children,
Unashamed
Spirit-sustainers.

Thank you.

Good Friday

I held her first at her baptism.
Even then she jigged and kicked
As if overcome
With delight.

Born to dance,
Matilda was now stilled
In the face of a drama
That spoke most deeply,
And disturbingly,
Within her blazing spirit.

Our congregation
Was reeling
At Christ's death
That Good Friday.

Adults were gasping,
Blinking back,
With more or less success,
Tears,
Some sobbing,
And a shroud of stillness
Enfolded us.

And she, now nineteen months,
Sat beside me,
Eyes fixed on the dance,
The dying,
In our midst,
Enthralled and mystified.

As, one by one, we rose,
Swallowing hard the grief,
She turned to her mother
Sharing, it seemed,
From depths to depths:
'Sad, Mummy!',
'Yes, darling, it's very sad.'

Spider's web

Some things are only gleaned
By the subtlest weaving
With the finest of all threads
In the dawn,
The gentlest
Most crazy
Exploring
In the heart.

A spider's web,
Tentative, dew-dipped
Dream's epitaph
So terribly vulnerable
To the rising sun
And to the wind,
Contains in its fragility
An awesome power.

Life is weaving webs.
More about adventure
Than certainty,
More about questions
And wonder
And finding our place in creation's delightful maze
Than about answers.

More about faith.

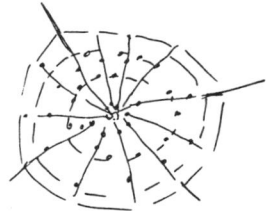

A harmony of the most enduring kind

She died this morning.

A long, haunting, single note
Flute like,
Clean,
Hangs in the air.

She had brought music,
Her great love and gift,
To many.

But now the long illness
Has taken its toll,
Thinking the music has died!

Not so!
A little
Of the world's most splendid,
Most gentle,
Music
Has faded,

But its echo
Grows stronger,
A blending harmony of the most
        enduring kind,
Ringing in our hearts
Grateful, enriched.

Jack

He had a flayed look,
A poverty
Borne of unspeakable things.

Gaunt,
In this new life
He taught in a boys' school.
A favourite trick:
To offer a miscreant
Either the cane, or a penny,
Mystifying all.

One day,
In the staff room before lessons,
He nearly impaled me
Against the door
Showing how in Changi,
Aged twenty,
He had learned knife-throwing.

Hints of one who has seen all,
Much more than can ever be told,
More than he ever wanted to remember;
Both his prison
And his hard, knowing, freedom.

At the age when we were driving
Our first Holdens and Volkswagens,
Brilliantine in our hair,
He had been skinning frogs in the jungle,
Body wracked with ulcers and malaria,
Mind slashed with the cruellest dreams,
Learning far deeper, more true,
Than we would ever
In our chase for credentials
That would certify our value
To the Department of Education.

They said you'd been a prisoner of war,
And now were plagued with injuries,
With a tendency to drink.

Thank you, Jack.

Soul friend

My strong, silent companion
Silver crest friend of the darkness
So long known by the ancient, leafless eucalypt
On the edge of the escarpment,
And the possum behind me.

Have you now gone?

Only an hour ago you were
That sliver of hidden orb's light
Hinting at greater strength
In the frosted night.

This planet's face,
Soul's mirror,
Brimful of passion, the quiet,
Bird-call, earthquake,
Birthing, dying.

Hardly aware of your massive
Tide-surge imprint
Always
Even when unseen in dawn glow.

Thank you

Soul friend.

THE
FLOWING

Tears

Now, having talked of tears,
They come
Gushing, uninvited.
Jaw, lip, cheeks trembling
In the outpouring of the self,
His whole body wracked with soul sobbing

Shaking his head slowly,
Sensing the flow wane,
Yet needing time for the spirit sap
To complete its flow,
He mops the salty smears
Spreading the wetness wider.

How ridiculous – trying to stop this miracle!

The residue of love's anointing
Leaves its cleansing dew all over,
And wayward splashes on his collar.

And sometime soon, he knew,
It would happen all over again,
Catching him with tissues in hand
Midway from his pocket.
This embarrassing gift,
Spirit filling each drop
In reverse baptism,
The life-giving flow from deep within
To eyelid, and spilling over,
Cascading really, down his face
To bathe another soul,
Healing oil for deepest wounds,
For those whose own tears are
Sadness salted with bitterness, only.

Refreshment

Some, in the name of helping another,
Succeed only in invading my space,
Crowding into my life with their agenda,
Inflicting their hurts and dreams
On my listening ears
Leaving me drained and hostile.

Others know how to be present
Lightly,
Giving room for my breathing,
To be,
To fill that space for a time
Blessed by the gift of their waiting
With me,
Spiced with the light
Dancing from their lips,
Their eyes,
Their gestures,
Their silence,
To my heart
For the healing.

*1 Corinthians 16:17, 18 'I rejoice
at the coming of Stephanas and
Fortunatus and Achaicus, be-
cause they have made up for your
absence, for they have refreshed
my spirit as well as yours. So give
recognition to such persons.'* (New
Revised Standard Version)

Rose garden

I smell them still,
Compassion, Chinatown, Kerassi, Little Joey,
Lovely Lady,
Bed upon bed where I have lingered,
Far too many to name them all.

So much beauty in one petal.
Compressed grace,
Too pungent to inbreathe deeply,
Too much for the eyes.

People everywhere
Wading slowly in this pool of colour,
Slowed by waves of perfumed grace,
With bees buzzing, bloated,
Cleansed in the richest aromas
Entirely.

Mary has washed our feet,
Too!

Luke 7:38 'She stood behind him at his feet, weeping, and began to bathe his feet with her tears and to dry them with her hair. Then she continued kissing his feet and anointing them with the ointment.' (New Revised Standard Version)

Water of affliction

Fruit of Mara
Promising greenness to barren spirits
But bearing pock-marks
To the soul.

How varied your form.
Masquerading,
Teasingly,
As Spirit-food light-filled
And sparkling with newness
But, in the tasting,
Grittedness.

And worse
In the mouths
Of those I love
And yearn to protect
From such inner agony.
For we all drink the one drink.

Only One greater than I can conceive
Could see the strengthening
In each dangerous droplet
Given, tearfully, your children,
Until Cana's gift,
The best wine,
Is poured.

Isaiah 30:20 'Though the Lord
may give you the bread of ad-
versity and the water of affliction,
yet your Teacher will not hide
himself any more, but your eyes
*shall see your Teacher.' (*New
Revised Standard Version*)*

Bougainvillea

Tropical red-heat in dry season,
Dust, wind, thirsting earth
Gasping for
One drop
Of life.

Sweet June-gift
Mauve, red, white
Colour bursts of festive delight
All crying 'Taste! Dance! Look! Receive!'
Scattering promise-laden pollen
Like the flooding Diamantina
To the south-east
Now many wide rivers
Destroying, renewing widely, with abandon.

Love is gushing water,
Is mauve, lilac, white, red
Splashes of life
In the dusky dryness.
Balm to eyes smarting with grit,
Coolness to thirsting lips,
Oases in the desert place.
Bougainvillea.

First sign, and last

One thing I was sure of,
I didn't come for this,
Launching into things
By fixing a catering problem
To keep the party rolling!

But she interfered
In her usual knowing way.
I told her 'No',
But she assumed I'd do as she desired.
And I did.

Looking back, there is no doubt
She knew the timing truer than I.
She, strong-spirited, knew the Creator's heart,
And six stone water jars gushed
Exotic wine.
Wine of joy!

As later, she was at my side
Knowing the ripeness of time again
When that other wine poured forth
Black wind screaming the air
Burning her heart
Grief-laden,
The best wine, the best wine,
Kept till agony's end.
Wine of peace!

Wine of joy,
Wine of peace,
Fruit of the love-crushing, the trampling,
Matured to the fulness
For all time.

John 2:1-11; 19:33-37

Water lily leaves

White flowering madonna's companions
Sun-bathed in autumn pond,
Holding in tension
Easily
Two realms.

Air – water;
Light – dark;
Clear – mysterious.

Not like the debris of wind-blown
tree-flotsam
Littering the waters messily.
Strangers to paradox,
Golden death hues water-washed thinly
In life's ebb
To rot utterly.
Denied Spring.

Soft circles of silent witness
At home in the stillpoint.
Embracing opposites effortlessly
As friends.

Holding apart without splitting
Linking in accepting peace
Simply
True wisdom nurture
For the flowering.

Pharisaic prison

Prison of glass,
Apparent freedom's centre
Clear, still fish-tank
White, brown and blue flecked tomb of life.

Water's flow throttled to tiny gasping bubbles
Fluid in right angles
Vertical walls of water!
Paralysed of mood and movement
Defying nature's surge impulse
To run amuck in bushland creeks
smashing bracken
trout-teeming
pounding rock gorges
slaking so many thirsts.

There on the mantelpiece
Frozen appearance of life
(Pity the sad prisoners, gold, silver and black
Trapped forever as by invisible steel
Doomed to endless slow circling
Amid brown-tinged weed)

Sweet stress reducer
Uptight, upright, unfree.

Snow

How those sunbathed mountains wept
Tenderly,
Discreetly.

Not like my heart-wrenched sobbing
As if stabbed to the core
By the sliver of stalactic ice in my hand,
Finger of cold light
Shot through with brilliant sun-flashed diamonds
Slashing the nerves with such pierced beauty.

A private grief
At last released,
Cascading,
Filling
The, 'til now, silent slopes.

Fresh fallen snow, now warming,
Mute echo of my cry.
Mirror of my dream,
Because of delicate beauty
Dissolving
As all true beauty must,
Destined for cyclic transformation.
Beyond preserving,
Of my heart, mind,
Now the moment of dissolution.

And snow cave stalactites
Each one in its grief dying
Drop by drop
Sent for this moment's so singular shedding
Of itself,
Fruit of the wider weeping.

And beyond,
Sun-brushed in red and gold,
Snow laden clouds offering
Replenishment.

Yet more myriads of dreams
To melt on the face,
Lavishing white grace
Everywhere.
For tomorrow's tears
Marking new more rich
Patterns in the soul.
New beauty
Beyond the dying.

The surf

There is a drawing power
In the sea
Calling the spirit to view,
Feel,
Pause,
Struggle
At its edges.

Lit with so many lights,
Throbbing with currents
That excite and alarm,
It calls
For repeated rites of homage
From tired land-locked spirits
Who know the limits
That grate and gouge,
And who urge
To defy them
By immersion,
Being pummelled by delicious wild powers
In that other realm.

PASSION

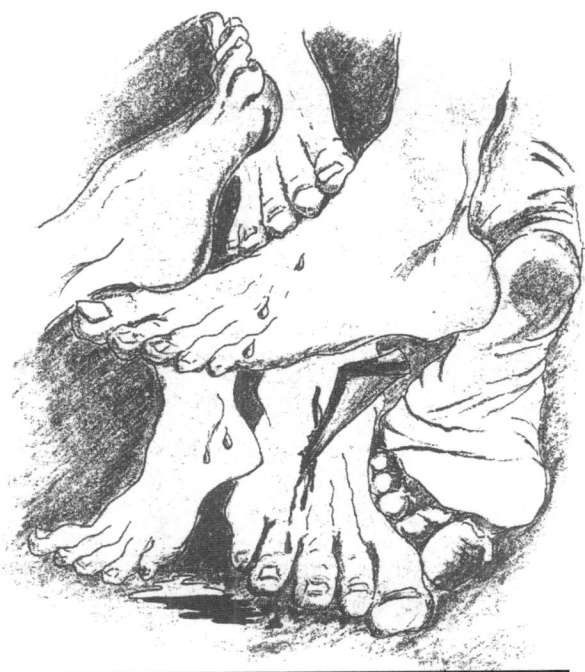

Passion I

I suppose he went there in his lunch hour
For the colours,
Between the rose beds,
Belching smoke from his pipe.

He, and others too, were washed
In waves of perfume,
But he didn't, wouldn't, know.
Such loving was beyond him,
Reaching for his tin of Dr Pat Medium Cut.

And Arkle and Southhampton and Belfast Lady
Would wait in vain
To touch noses with him.
A shame, with summer racing by,
Not much time left
Before the thorns
Grow sharper.

Jerusalem, Jerusalem,
How I have yearned to in-
gather your children,
as a hen gathers her chicks
under her wings, and you
refused.'
Matthew 23:37-39

Passion II

She, in a ludicrous emotional outburst
Of generosity,
Poured expensive perfume on his head!
He, blinking it from his eyes,
Inhaled,
Reeking of beauty.

And, seeing her heart,
He accepted her offering
For his death
And the wordless, endless fragrance
Of her love.

Matthew 26:6-13

Passion III

A dark, black hole
Sucked, splintered
Goodness into oblivion.
Judas felt food
Sticking
In his throat,
Lumping in his chest,
And gulped, noisily, a draught of red wine
Before excusing himself from dinner.

He had an appointment.

He would sell him to religious men
Who knew what they were about.
They would rid him, and them,
Of the One whose candour,
Like litmus,
Had exposed a dark deep spirit acid within
Judas.
And which, in the loving,
Would tear away
In screams
His very life.

Matthew 26:14-16, 20-25
Acts 1:16-20

Passion IV

Not only Judas,
Stained beyond wanting cleansing,
Left him that night.

They all did.

He would have loved their company
After his last meal with them.
Facing the final bread breaking,
The last wine outpouring.
They could have steeled his heart
With their presence.

Despite their pledges,
They, even Peter, fled
In their confusion
Brutalising him
More
Than soldiers' spittle, or spike, or spear.

Matthew 26:26-35

83

Passion V

A kiss may be an act of passion
Or a greeting of affection.
Or it may disguise the deepest guilt
Of other loves,
A thing of cold, cold lips,
Averted eyes,
Hurried.

Judas, in that embrace,
Betrayed not Jesus,
But himself
As Jesus' foe.
Heard those final wounding words,
Jesus whisper low,
'My friend!'

Matthew 26:47-50

Passion VI

Gnarled olive trees and sighing wind
Gave leave to prancing horrid things
Taunting, haunting, joining
Inner beast in dirge-like song
Seen, heard, felt by Jesus
Only.

His friends slept.

His nightmare
Was beyond them
In this garden of shadows.
As drugged, their bodies slumped,
Eyes closed,
While his battle raged
Nearby.

His heart breaking,
Three times he found them sleeping.
On this journey of searing spirit,
Across this wilderness,
They could not go.

He would tread this path alone,
Wrestle and sob and bleed without their aid
Or knowing,
Beg and plead for another way,
Then, drink the cup while shadows shrieked.

'And now', he said, 'You can take your rest'.

Mark 14:32-42

Passion VII

The soldier's lone foolish trophy
Was the youngster's underpants,
All he was wearing
When they tore the darkness
Flaying, if they could,
The Light.

They had grabbed him
Thrown him,
Vented their rage at him,
As he made for the trees
And fled their feeble torches
(Sickly signs of their flickering spirits,
Cowards, armed to the teeth,
Seeking to silence an unarmed agitator).

But they had their prize!
His friends escaped Rome's clutches,
But not Jesus.

And now he acted as if he had found them,
Rather than they, him!
As if he were leading them,
The centre of that moving circle
Clanking awkwardly, ridiculously,
Like small boys at a dress-up party,
All the way to the High Priest's house.

And blushing,
One with some underpants
Stuffed in his belt.

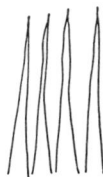

Mark 14:43-52

Passion VIII

He washed his hands dramatically,
With flair,
A public gesture of dismissal,
But felt the symbol hollow,
Not removing,
But inflaming,
His guilt.

'My dear', he said at dinner,
Dabbing wine from his chin,
'What else could I do? I feared violence!'

No matter how he drank and walked and talked
that night
Seeking to shift the weight in his soul,
Pilate's wife saw the torment curdling his brain,
Souring the semblance of wisdom.
He now knew the one whose dream-touch
Had swept her soul
Had leapt, forever, to his.

He did, however,
Allow a decent burial,
Hoping to get rid
Of the evidence.

Matthew 27:11-26

Passion IX

Wounded grief.
These women loved him,
Had been healed, renewed by him,
And followed at a distance
Each tortured step,
Felt with him the nails, thorn, spear,
The scoffing and the jeering.

They had been close to him,
And cared for him.
Now, in their tears,
They could only watch his dying,
Mourn at his tomb,
Live dark long hours
With no consoling hand like his —
Their men having fled in fear —
Their loving deeper, truer, stronger yet.

Matthew 26:55, 56

Passion X

He could give nothing
But his own tomb
Feeling no consolation
For his grief.

The One he had followed,
Planted life in Joseph's heart,
A dream, a strength,
Was dead.

Confronting Pilate,
He tenderly
Reversed that crucifixion,
Removing nails, thorns,
Cleaning wounds,
Replacing derision with dignity
Wrapped in the cleanest and softest of shrouds.

And Jesus' face and feet,
Washed again with tears of love
Confused, angry, deep,

Freed of strain and sweat
At last,

Awaiting angel's touch.

Matthew 26:57-61

COMING

Advent

The Powerful Unexpected
Beyond our dreaming,
Planning,
Our predicting.
Far, far beyond our imagining
(No God-in-a-box, tinsel and card
'O, thank you, just what I always wanted!'
Said with a giggle).

God has not come in this manner
But will.
Certainly.

Beyond summer-winter cycle
More certain than
Seed-to-flower miracle,
More full than fruit, ripening deathward

Leaping from cosmic splendour,
Regal, with fragile, beauteous strength.
Bathed in love.

All-transforming.

Matthew 24:36-44

That birth

No angels, no star, for her:
Nothing more than that simple, agonising
miracle –
The agent of all creation
Gulps air and cries
And struggles, kicking, for the breast,
God compressed into the tiniest,
Most fragile human form.

Others saw and heard the heavens move
That night
And gasped
And rushed to look.
But for the mother of God
Nothing could ever adorn this birth,
Impress it more deeply.
She would see the maturing
And await the making and the breaking
Of God,
Pondering that flesh,
Listening to that spirit
Beckoning along the path
Of a most winsome,
Most delicate
Peace.

'Blessed are those whose fragility is strength,
And whose strength is fragile.'

Luke 2:1-10

The shining

Soft candle flicker
Life's breath
Lighting loaf, cup,
Table, people
So tenderly
And bathing all so richly.
Enveloping Presence.

Soft greyness, fog-laden,
All penetrating in morning's dampness.

Brilliant eye-squinting glare
Retina stab
Of open road, of concrete strip, of dry sands.
Burning summer laser.

Rippler of ocean bed
Through multiform refracting filters,
Dancing and weaving through watery lenses
Slow motion caresser of that world
Of mystery, beauty and bones
All fearfully magnified
In your magic slanting rays.

Glinting of planet and star,
Reflected moon ambience
In galaxies untold,
Self-giving life force
Since baptising this world
In creation's dawn.
But secreted in glow worm
And phosphorescent splash
Fleetingly.

How sweeping your touch,
Yet so subtle.

At home
More than us
In the universe.
At home in the shining
Burning soul fire
Incense flung free.

Shine, Jesus, shine!

Elusive One

Where are you, sweet Jesus?

The two businessmen sat in the restaurant
Enjoying a two-hour dialogue
On global economics,
German and Indonesian jousting
In the Darwin heat
Rudely
Ignoring almost completely the elderly man
Seated between them.
A white man, knowing the words they used
But no meaning, looking at plate, cutlery,
hanging ferns,
Averted gaze of one rejected
His feelings frozen (out of habit?)
Like the ice in his consoling drink.
Who, mid-way, paused when returning from the
salad bar,
And said to me gently, almost whimsically,
Spirit to spirit (my table, too, offered no
companionship)
'Are you a regular here?'

Where are you, sweet Jesus?

In the warm night air the rescue services
Haul him in a sling, drunk, limp, like
flesh-sack
From the rock ledge where he had stumbled, screaming
And tend him gently at cliff's edge in the ambulance
Under palm trees moaning in the wind.
While fan-cooled, the choir
Perspire their next Sunday's offering, love-filled.

Where are you, sweet Jesus?

It's a beautiful building
Locked almost all week
For occasional use for non-Aboriginal folk,
So it seems —
Those who have the key.
They enjoy the beauty of holy space,
Green decorative plants,
Symbols that inspire, are treasured.
But most nights, dark folk gratefully sleep,
Having no right of entry,
Under the eaves
And one even slept in the porch
Last hot Sunday afternoon.

Where are you, sweet Jesus?

Keep me from bitter judgment,
Open to sweetness of Spirit-fruit,
Love spiced,
Energised by tears, scream,
Thin trickle of dark red blood
Spilt on hot Golgotha soil,
Flesh-sack on nails.

True sweetness
Searing and graced.

Sunrise

You come with a thousand voices
Filling the sky with quadraphonic sound
Displacing the baying and haunting sounds of
darkness.
Birdcalls ring the earth,
Wringing it and us from the slowness of
slumber.

You come in the pale chill
Of early morning
With a pristine brilliance
Wet with new birth
Splashed with the memory of creation's dawn.

You come to renew,
Warming the cold soil softly
With a painful tenderness,
Enfolding and lightening its creatures
For the living of a new day.

You come, so welcome friend for the troubled
Proclaiming that night is not the end,
Melting the frost,
Burning the fog,
Hope bearer for those slowed and numbed
By pain.

You come,
Bathing our aching limbs
Spiriting our flagging souls,
For the new.

Thank you,
Cyclic, relentless breather of new life,
Of new days and new vistas,
Marking our living
With fresh sown seeds of waking light,
Signs of a yet fuller, warmer Glow.

*Genesis 32:31 'The sun rose above
(Jacob) as he passed Peniel, and
he was limping because of his hip'.*
(Revised Standard Version)

Those sighs haunt

Those sighs haunt.
The sighing of Jesus at Lazarus' death,
Of grief, a heart torn open,
Of love, for a friend now gone.

The cry of God in the face of our dying
The soft face of God for a hardening world,
Creator anguish at the tearing of fibres.
The smell of death on the planet –
Emotional, nuclear, chemical,
Religious, economic, political,
Self-centred sepulchres,
Killing fields
For the fruit of all violence,
The end-point of dreams.

The sighing of God is in the wind-swept trees,
and the call is coming,
The boughs breaking,
The grave-clothes tearing,
The stones are rolling away
At the sound of it all.

There is a stripping of fetters,
A shredding,
A tearing of unfreedoms.

These are the sighs that haunt,
Fanning the fire within
Of a conviction
There is a place called hope.

John 11:33, 38-44

Battered and bruised

Battered and bruised
He winced
At the impact:
The Baptist had been beheaded
In a distant cold fortress
To entertain
The mother of a strip-tease star.

Destroyed was he
Who had prepared for him
With such courage
In the wildest places
The Way.

Hungry for solitude,
He left followers and crowds
All replete
At day's end,
And retreated
In that hard and lonely place
To the famine of his own desert storm.

This, this is the Way
John had paved
In his bold, brash manner,

This, this is the storm;
The wrestling in a deserted place
Echoing with the cries of roaming beasts
Hungry to devour the humble,
Vulnerable, spirit,
Of that earlier wrestle,
Fresh from baptism by this same John.

This, this is the place
Of tears,
Of the flinging of questions
And the framing of options
And of arguing with Self
And Satan
And God,
Under that cold black sky
Studded with stars
Burning into his soul.

This, this is the oasis,
Healing of pain,
Seeing clear-eyed
Strongly again
With the ebbing of the weakness of grief

And in seeing is cut to the quick
By his disciple's dismay
And leaves his own storm
For theirs.

Out of his new-found peace
He must address
The darkest powers
Raging those treacherous waters
   – Yes, he must walk
     On water!

And Peter
Must also make
That crazy, crazed leap
Into the abyss
To sink and to be held
In the arms of such great,
Such tender strength,
To be carried,
Strong fisherman,
Filled with fear,
By a carpenter.
Consoled by the One
Who knows better than most
Storm and peace,
And who will take again
Into his own soul
The Terror
In greater measure,
For the spreading
Of Shalom
For many who will to be carried
Over the waters.

Matthew 14:13, 14, 22-33

Narrowly it comes

How narrowly
The Word comes
Like a splinter unexpected
As splinters always are,
How cleanly to the nerve
It slices
Even for pilgrims
Who say
They are eager
To hear,
Straining with all ears
And faces all aglow
To catch each word
Spoken by this Son of Joseph.

How sickening
The unwanted lance
Exposing a sense of dread
Of the darkest kind,
Quickly turning the heart
From sheer joy

— What honeyed words,
    From one of our own, too,
    Our own bright god,
    Ours to claim
    And ours to boast,
    Sweetness beyond belief!

                        ...To rage!

This Word, he says,
Will not be heard
Here,
Will ricochet from mind and heart
Utterly,
Leaving scarce a mark
Except hostility that this should be,
And a screaming for the silencing
Of this most inly voice.

O selective, divine permeation,
This choice and choosing grace,
Don't,
Please,
Pass by
This place,
This space,
My self.

Luke 4:14-30

SECRETS

The leaf

An awful, ordinary moment
Of parting.
A single maple leaf
Gently detached from its life-source.

A soft, necessary dying,
A goodbye to the past life
Of giving
To the tree.

Now, fully given,
Freed to dance the wind
Splashing the air with such wild redness
Dappled dancing
In whirls and spirals,
Fits and starts,
Leaving, almost, dashes of colour
Suspended yet in motion,
For the memory.

Beyond sunset

Cold, vermilion smudged wisps
Flower-splashed beyond richness
Light piercing blue backdrop immense –
So still, yet surely, slow-swift, changing.

And gnarled eucalypt,
Lone, broken sentry
Guarding the spectre through time,
Changelessness etched against fluid sky,
A magic
Framed
Momentarily
For the senses.
Stark, black silhouette,
Frozen death,
Brilliant hues beyond.

Colours stream by,
Darker
Yet darker
Flow.
Miracle missed by averted gaze,
Even fleetingly,
(Cold, bleak cigarette-ash grey of death).

One solitary evening star
Jewelled in wonder,
Precious hope amid ice-blue and grey.
Fresh light!
Sunset's death in new dawn's taste
Received in gratitude.

A most ancient crying

In the bush breezes
Is a sliver of sound
That has the effect
Of walking over a dead man's grave.
A hint only
Of a painfilled past
Seen in the banksia
Obliquely
At best.

Europeans love Floriade's
Extroverted brilliance –
Tulips, daffodils, petunias –
Artistry of the most ordered kind,
And blatant,
With Devonshire Teas
And canned music
Between riots of colour.

But Australia's past
Is enshrined and extolled
In a mysterious
Eerie
Quietness
That shows itself coyly
With the beauty of reticence,
Requiring the courage to hear
Stories of wonder dressed
In a most primitive garb,
And shy.

Stories told only to hearts
Open to mystery,
Ears willing to hear
What lies behind
The shadows.
Stories of spirits
And knowing
From the dreaming.

A deep, deep lament
In the soul
And the soil
Of this land.
Like banksia-men
Punctured
Weirdly
And thorned
In yesterday's
Flowering.

Nature's lacerated memory
Taunting and haunting
For all time
Those who say
They love this land.

'Banksia' – Australian flowering bush shrub or tree

'Banksia-men' – name given to the dark coloured, ugly shaped pods of the banksia

Jacob

Jaded Jacob,
Muddied with anxiety,
Trod to Jabbok's clear flow
To wrestle.

Bearer of lust's seed
Grasping into piddling piles
Things,
As if enough of them make life,
And yet more of them make life full and free,

He fell.

Pebbles, weeds, surging spirit
Pummelled him in the darkness.
Gasping, he felt the strength of
Another,
Who knew pain deeper yet,
Had seen the crack in Jacob's heart,
The gleam in his eye
Of questing,
Begging for fragrance, light,
Burning for love.

Disbeliever at heart
Of the myth he lived by,
This solitary soul sought points of fire
unknown,
So thrashed and screamed 'til he won,

Aching with love
And pain
He danced the dance
Of one who has truly
Been pummelled,
A shaken, ashen thing

Inbreathed,
Free,
Having gained all
At that cool, dark river
By silent eucalypts

Tears brimming with the sweetest light,
Beyond dreaming.

Genesis 32, 33

Sacred places

Bare feet I saw
Briefly framed in the bus window.
Pink dress, yellow shorts, blue shirt
Hair wet shampoo smelling
        – children of sparkling ebony, barefoot
dancing to school.

I heard the stories at Nungalinya:

'My people chained to rocks, trees,
Flogged, flayed to dark redness.
Maybe hundreds. Near Wyndham'.

'White kids would hit me with a stick
When I ate my sandwich sometimes. No reason.'

'"Say – did you hear about that drunk gin
Hit by a car like a dead kangaroo?"
She was my aunt. Don't you say that.
"Oh, not you, I just thought it was funny,
that's all"'.

'We had to scrub the floors
If we couldn't remember a Bible verse
Or something'.

'Funny how we used to wear dresses
Made of hessian,
And sew a white man's singlet at the crotch for bathers.
Funny, that'.

'That pool there was covered,
Covered with their blood'.

Sacred places everywhere.
Will bare feet be nail rid?
Will the bleeding ever cease,
Tender child's feet be washed,
Massaged with love –
Innocent holiness with justice
In this gibbet-strung land?

Darwin, Northern Territory

Sailing I

What surging magnetism
Draws me to those wind-whipped waves?
Why so powerful the call to sail to the limits
And, occasionally, beyond them?
Hull's lift, stabbing thrust
Of freshly wind-gust empowered cat
Slicing the waters open
Roaring, crashing spray
Almost capsizing.

I need the fight,
Wet wind-slapped face,
Sore muscles.

I polish the hulls for yet more speed
(Past risks insuffice)
Driven deeply to place my body
Closer to the elements
That would claim me.

Is sailing my pilgrimage
Of fright/joy
And the lake
My Mother, painfully beautiful
And sweetly, darkly possessive?
Never, in the depths,
Truly contented.
Always harbouring a rising storm
Today – next week –
Is this the source of threat
To which I am drawn?
An addict to the restless power
I so need
But which awakens my fear?

For that wind, those waves, those forces
Are within
Most stormy,
My baptism
Mirrored in each lake storm.

Sailing II

It seems as if you have sent me
Away,
As if you think I need a break – and you too –
From your enfolding.
At your bidding I go
To waves, wind, and thick, thick darkness.

I had thought the presence of friends
Enough.
But fear steals subtly, then,
Whipped by fever,
Rages all night
Tosses and washes me like stranded kelp in
the surf,
The darkening surf.
Like when I was drowning that day, aged six,
Lungs screaming for air, sucking salt water
Only.
To be pumped out later by strangers,
Limp and spluttering sickly on the sand.

I said I would never surf again
– My new credo –
And I didn't, the next day.
(Was that you, over there, smiling at my vow?)

Even if you bear me terror,
You come.
Fear of you will change
Again to trust,
You who strides through spirit storms within
As if they, too,
Are yours!

Matthew 14:22-33

Sailing III

Spirit storms are the eeriest of things:
Empowering winds take new, stark forms,
A wildness that could break life and limb
In unforgiving foam.
They can bear much bitterness or
With your aroma-touch,
Not.

In the ebb and flow come
Dangerous Marah things
Taunting and haunting
The soul
While the Creator withdraws a space
For tea
(Yes, it is hard work
In a sea of pain.
But God has been called briefly away!)

Wind drops,
Waves wash gentle spirit things,
Subtly scenting the nostrils,
Visioning eyesight
With soothing springs and shady palms
Not of Las Vegas,
But of Elim.

Exodus 15:22-27;
Matthew 14:22-33

119

Sailing IV

Raging, chopping, changing winds
Will reduce you
In the end
To new depths of humility.

Sometimes it is right
And necessary
To be overcome
After adrenalin surge
And searing pace;
To be stilled, mastered, silenced
In a soggy heap,
Bruised and blue,
Searching for a way out,
The way back
To the beach.

Discovering the limits
Is as crucial, it may be,
For the freeing of the self,
As relishing
Strengths.

Sailing V

Perhaps it was because he heard
What lay behind
My broken words,
The rawness dammed,
Welling yet contained,
That he offered,
Later,
To take me sailing
On the estuary.

Perhaps he, also,
Knew the inly grief
Of a groaning
Deeper than tears
For a loved one
Whose dream had died:
The stabbing ache
In the heart
Of the heat
Of another's desert.

And so he comforted me
In the simplest
And surest
Of ways.

And wind slashed,
Salt spattered on the wild Swan
We came ashore,
Drank coffee,
And relished the cleansing
By that strong sail slapping
Fremantle doctor.

'Swan': Swan River, Western Australia

'Fremantle doctor': local name given the strong westerly winds that frequently blow from Fremantle across Perth, Western Australia

Pregnancy

She fled, hardly believing,
To her cousin in the hills.
And knowledge beyond words
Passed between them,
Touching the embryo
Of the one who would
Always respond to you in the flesh.
And Elizabeth understood
The Spirit had brushed her
In that coming.
She knew, as a woman might,
Of the fruit being formed
In her cousin's womb,
Could see the tears
Of hope and young fear
In those unforgettable eyes.

And perhaps both knew their offspring,
Bone, flesh and spirit of theirs,
Sparkling and burning and igniting hope,
Would die early, and John first.

Sweet, deep pain,
As ever,
Of woman's joy and grief
Who bears a child
For freedom.

Luke 1:39-56

They weren't to know

This mere boy from a most insignificant town
– Nothing great came from it, some said –
Amazed them,
Astounded them with a wisdom
Beyond their learning.

Little did they know
Their life was in his hands.
Soon, they would be the children, plying
questions,
Full of learning yet empty,
Searching for the love
That would break him.

Then the Temple would be shaken,
Their world erupt in havoc,
Veil tear, graves open, darkness fall,
And some would search for him in days to come
And beg of him to hear them,
Hand in hand with fishermen and prostitutes
And crowds of others, kneeling,
– About his Father's business,
    He had said!

Luke 2:41-50

She trembled in Nazareth

Newly tasting
The thrill and fear
Of adulthood,
She trembled
In Nazareth.

Exploring and enjoying
Her love of Joseph,
Mary dreamed of marriage,
Of love, of children
By that strong,
Rough carpenter.

But into her world of hope
And ecstasy
Came Gabriel,
Instrument of grace
And perplexity.

She trembled
In Nazareth
Because she knew
Not only flesh-love,
But this spirit warmth,
Hers in so focused a flame
That the miracle of her womb
Would touch and change her life,
And ours,
As no other.

She trembled
In Nazareth
For the holy
Danced in her heart.

With a strong light
Burning in brown eyes,
She surrendered her being
To the bearing
And the sharing
Of a fleshly
Bright God
In Bethlehem's stable;
Warm centre of a wintered world.
And to giving his body her breast
And his spirit her strength,
For the birthing in others
Of fruit imperishable.

Luke 1:26-38

Anniversary

You died prematurely,
Taking us all by surprise.
Your final wound too deep,
And Mrs Foley found your body,
Called the police.

You never knew the girl who became my wife,
My children,
My path in life
That has led me closer to your pain
In others,
And in my own self.

You knew hard beginnings,
Loss of reputation and dream,
Great deprivation.

Your ideas collapsed in on themselves
And you turned frenetically to gardening,
Desperately trying to bury your anger
Unsuccessfully,
Face reddened and gasping for air.

Could no-one get close to you?
Glimpse for a moment
The brute power of your weeping?
See the twisted hurt in your soul?
(It was too much for me,
Even as you rested, on show,
In the casket
That winter's afternoon.)

You trod the lonely path
Of many who are highly gifted,
Misunderstood,
Doing good wherever you were able.

And many you met were wounded
In your frenzy for love.
You most of all.

I see you, love you,
As never before.

A little dying

A little dying
Hurts everyone
Deeply.

The question is:
How best to learn
That life is more
About letting go
Than about other things?

Some of the truest learning
Seems to flow
From a surrendering
Of a dream,
The forgoing of an opportunity
That once seemed a necessary goal.

A seminary official told my friend
Who was withdrawing from studies,
'Bob, some of our very best students
Never graduate!'

For life is about
Brushing against others
So as to colour their lives a little
With a bloom,
Even the most fragile hue.

As lines gouged by the years of knowing
On an aged person's face
But leaving a dancing twinkle in the eye,
What is diminished in me
Moulds and refashions the spirit,
In the ways
Of the deepest wisdom.

Retirement

Season of completion,
Of fulfilment,
Living the dreams
Long held, long nourished.
Of reading, walking, sight-seeing,
Loving, meditating, treasuring
Particular friendships,
Special past-times.
Of hobbies long postponed
Or yet to be developed
And relished.

But also the season of many griefs,
Of bereavement, illness,
Declining powers,
And the slow seeping of a pain
Beyond words
Deep.

The time of fuller flowering
Of long-present, half-hidden
Shadows
Released with declining inhibitions,
Both inflicting pain and triggering delirious
delight
In relative and friend.

Season of enigma
Of a strong wisdom
Flickering in the sometimes fading memories,
And brimful of promise
For the spirit
Newly empowered
For the other, closer, place.

The two faces of Horeb

Fresh from God's hand
They glowed
Drawing the heart
To the Source
Beyond all.

Gifts, signs, tokens
Of freedom,
New directions,
Sparkling with promise.

But now they melt
In hideous heat
And reform
To another pattern,
Beast of gold.

How do I truly think
To find life
In the clever, prayerful
Constructions of my piety,
The carefully honed
Fruit and gifts
Of the Spirit,
The precious, crafted offerings
Even,
Of love?

Holy ground
And burning bush
Twist and turn
To birth monstrous shapes,
Desecrated,
Hollow,
Of the void,
Scarring the face
Of the Mountain of God.

Lord, help me to grind
To finest dust
Such images of self
And all perverted portrayals
Of you,
All images of deceit
In my soul,
Tawdry, insubstantial things,
My self-imprint,
And scatter all,
All,
On the waters.

Exodus 32:1-24

Poisoned chalice

He sat
Clutching the pain within,
Nursing the hollowed
Hurt
In his belly.

For years he had skirted around
With his intellect
Or with games
That appalling space,
Distracting
But always avoiding
The blackness,
Repulsed by his own repulsion.

And that numbing, searing
Unspeakable poison
Tainted all,
Leaving a tarnished and soured replica only
Of vintage wine.

With what courage
Is the awesome fouling
Faced.

Pandanus

Ungainly pain
Heat-snapped in the burning
Agony beyond telling
The twisted disjointed image
Of nature's crucifixion.
Form without form
As if created in fright.
Fits and starts of being
Hiroshima print of life fragmented
Intended
Framed in delicate compassion,
Gentle breeze caressed,
Full of promise
Hidden in black.

But higher,
Miracle-green shoots
Savage, wild beauty
Fire of life green-flamed
Ever burning
Firm flaring
Healing amid the brutal tearing purging
Tears
White hot.

Seeing in the spaces

How quietly they may speak
Their heart.
Fragile shafts of self-light,
Delicate shimmering spirit stuff
In word, look, pause.
Listen closely, white man, listen.

How smoothly darting are the all-seeing eyes
Probing deeply,
Weighing mysteries beyond our cluttered world
Of things, logic, reason.

You have come to learn:
Learn, then, in the fullness of the spaces
Not facts, features,
History's record of what we've done to them.
Listen to the hesitation of those who
remember
And whose memories are soaked in pain
Beyond telling.
The memories of those who know crucifixion
Better than we will ever know wood,
Nails, whip, power abused
In mortifying flesh, mind, spirit
Without end.
Look for meaning between the lines
Of our angular, stilted world
Of form-wrapped emptiness.
And beyond,
Free visions
Of that bright other sphere
Scarcely touching what is in our world given.

Empty-seeming only
Spaces of time, thought, life-shapes
In the mid-point
Distilled essence undreamt
Of the dreaming.
(I'd never met Wali's brother before
Fresh from the bush,
But he said he had known me.
Perhaps he had, in his tear-stained knowing.
Perhaps he had.)

Fuller truth than our intellect can grasp
Red ochre wisdom-soaked
Spirit-filled from old,
Fruit of this land.

See the teeming boundless fulness
In spaces
Once thought, foolishly,
Pools of nothingness.

Written on retreat with Australian Aborigines in Darwin, Northern Territory

When dreams crumble

How does this God
Who allows dreams to crumble
And death
Wreak havoc
On a cross

Keep, hold, harness
Anything?

Where is there safety
In a God who tastes dying
Daily?

I would grasp,
If I could,
Such a power
That draws lines
Gently
Through battered time,
Space,
Heart,
Cords of love
To bandage the bleeding,
Echoes of peace
Inside the screaming,
Holding all in a pattern
Of profound, chaotic strength
That rings out across the universe
A music,
Catching every melody,
Each possible harmony,
In every variation,
Weaving each and every sound
Into the score,
Undoubtedly composed!

Fruit of One
Who knows
Far more than I can guess
Dying
And life.

Psalm 121

*Colossians 1:16, 17 '...for in him all things in heaven and on earth were created, things visible and invisible, whether thrones or dominions or rulers or powers – all things have been created through him and for him. He himself is before all things, and in him all things hold together.' (*New Revised Standard Version*)*

Silence of God

Whose silence is this?
When the searching spirit
Begs and pleads
For a sign
That its cries have been heard?

More awful than my own silence
Is this.
The silence of God.
When the Divine
Does not need to speak
Or rend the heavens
And the earth.

As if the Spirit
Retreats
And refuses
Even the most anguished
Love-filled cry,
The deepest longing
For that appearing
That alone surely would satisfy
The traveller.

As if God
Has evaporated,
Leaving not a trace.
A ghostly,
Ghastly,
Absence.

And faith is stretched
In ways thought impossible.

Not like the testing
Of the burning heat
And icy cold
Of the wilderness,
Where the test
At least
Is proof
Of the Other,

This silence
Signifies
Nothing,
No-one.

A darkness
Severe,
Lifting only
When the faithing
Has found new depths
Of horror
And of beauty.

1 King's 19:1-19

The embryo

To be utterly and serenely agnostic
Of what is beyond,
Cannot be predicted,
Shape and form
Beyond dreaming,
Is a profound
And wonderful
Gift.

Believing
That all is guided
By a Power,
Moved by a Love,
Seeded
And destined to mature.

Not claiming
But surrendering
The need to know
Final things
– Shape, outcome,
    Design, pace.

A greater knowing,
A deeper, truer, wisdom.

Seeing in the embryo,
Not full, final form,
The miracle:
Bursting with patterns,
Traces, wisps,
Of life
Though hidden
For a time,
Awaiting,
Always awaiting
With a twinkling of eye,

Birth.

Hebrews 11:1

TIMING

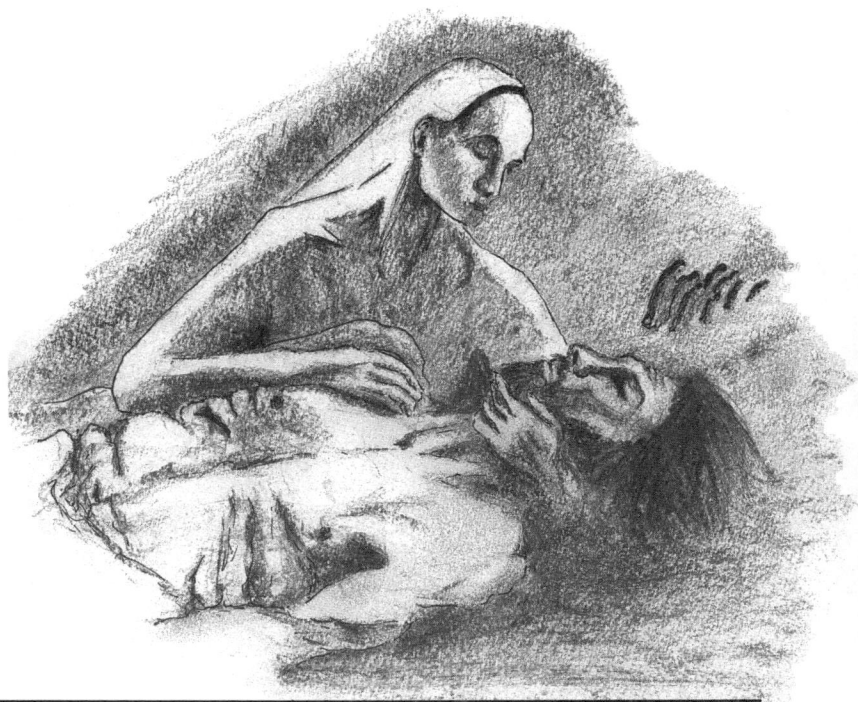

Winter

Season of slowness,
Of pausing, reflecting.

Season of contemplation,
Drawing on the sap of past gifts and graces.
Dreaming of tomorrow's Spring,
Shrugging off learnings discarded,
Dry leaves of Autumn.

Daring to be open to light
To nurture
Yet unseen growth,
Of the most quiet kind,
The hope of the thawing, green shoots, the
budding

Fresh warmings of the Spirit.

Darkness

Some darkness
Is necessary.

As shadows,
One by one,
Fell long ago
In Jerusalem
On that loneliest God.

Falling,
Falling,
Falling to the sighs of cypresses
Bending in a chill wind,
And the soft, mournful cry
Of an owl,

So I kneel
In my Gethsemane
And pray the dawn
That will not,
Must not,
Come.

And despite my grief-sobbed
Cries,
Each shadow
Banishes every hint of light.

Dawn will not hasten.
Light-laced dreams abide their time;
For come in healing splendour
They will,

The boil lanced,
The pain allowed to steal away

In time.

John 12:27

Second half of life

Winter is resting,
All of life
Taking a nap.

Winter is the second half
Of life
After the Spring and Summer
Of first birth
And joyous fruitfulness.

Lying low,
Savouring paucity for a time,
Mellowing,
Processing life's compost,
Draining the cup of richest
Autumn colours
To the dregs
Carefully, not wasting a drop.

For new births
Of the most intense
And knowing
Kind.

Winter's morning

Invisible waves of truth
Criss-cross the so-still air
And penetrate
The soul
Long before sun's rays.

I am swept
Through
By Spirit-rays
Pinpointing
Clearly
The smallest of black icicles
Lurking under the surface
On the inside.

And the darkness
Hidden even from my eyes,
Like frozen mud
On the edges of a pond,
Is
Lit!

And truth,
Hurtfully,
Becomes crystallised grace
With morning's frost face
Bearing beauty out of black barrenness
On every grass blade,
Every twig,
Each tiny leaf,
The so-white imprint
Of a transformation
That is winter's lavish gift.

Psalm 139:1-18

Spring

We should celebrate
This wildest
Erupting
In Spring.

With colours recklessly splashed everywhere
In this the season of new
Daily episodes
Of wonder
And delight.
Autumn is turned on its head:
Not the richness of life's ebbing,
But buds bursting
Hearts thirsting
Green shoots on grey branches
Marking
Not the end,
But a million points
Of the transforming
Of earth.

And even the soil
Smells
Newly
The promise.

After the dying
The fading
The crying
The slowing of the living
Winter's imperceptible crawl,
The freezing of sap and sinew
And the shrivelling and hollowing of hope
Comes Another
From the brilliant far side
Of Death.

Breathing into the dying,
Sparking fires of love
In hate-darkened, frosted hearts,
Flames of hope
For the greyness,
A gleam of a dream
In the scarred, battered spirit.

And the most free inhaling
Of friendly fresh air
Requiring no withdrawing,
Rubbing of blued hands
And curling in blankets.

With an unfolding
For the budding
Of the self
Where it was never
Expected.

Some call it
Resurrection.

Matthew 28:1-9

Summer eucalpyt

Stripped in heat wind
Soft grey sheets
Snapping, shedding, quilting the earth
Lavishly.

Exposing smooth cream gentleness
Like youth flesh,
Full, sweet, innocent,
Eucalypt limbs of beauty beyond speech.
Delicate new-born promise
Soon to be pain-filled,
Slashed, torn by stabbing beak,
Scribbled scrawl deep-written in flesh,
Nature's other tongues
Displayed for all to read
And wonder.

Scarred
Until the final wrench
Next hot summer
When growth will again demand
Death.

And then,
Above the fresh shredded shrouds
Trodden underfoot,
Windblown,
Beauty will again shine.
As on that other Tree,
Exposed in splendour
Swaying in regal praise
Death's exquisite fruit,
Pledge of transformation
In the breaking.

The Nunc Dimittis

Could I ever have Simeon's peace?
Be able to say:

It is over.
I am grateful and fulfilled.
All I ever wanted, Lord,
Has been granted.
And far, far more than my accomplishments
Is that Spirit-sheen,
The gift of your hands,
Which alone allows me
To turn and see your beckoning.

My friend, with cancer raging,
Could say it
His best work, he knew, was done,
And he saw, held, his first grandchild.
For all his regrets,
He knew at last your Spirit-call
And drifted away to you,
Leaving us to ruin our shoes
In the holy graveside mud.

I pray I could say it,
Know the time,
Have eyes to see, heart to know
That another day, week, year
Would not be gifts, but burden,
Stretching the living across deserts of pain,
Labouring the point of my existence
To exhaustion,
Delaying the completion,

And bruising,
Bruising my companions.

Why postpone the party, if all is prepared?

Luke 2:25-32

Lazarus

I had hoped he would spend some time with me
Yesterday, morning or afternoon,
But it isn't to be until today.

I should be used to waiting
I've been sailing so often.
Preferably, I have always thought spiritual direction
Should be on tap
Iced, sparking, ready to go when required.

Waiting, it seems
Has its own value.
Like last Monday,
Waiting for my first meeting with him,
In the shade of the church porch
With the shimmering tropical heat of car park, palms,
And two Australian Aborigines
One reading a newspaper, the other,
Squatting, smoking and sipping a drink.
They seemed to know how to wait.
At ease.
Accepting time's flow.
Savouring its taste.
Missing nothing, rushing nowhere, deeply attentive.
I was to wait five hours that day, and spent the time
Frantically devouring books.

How hard comes the waiting,
The plane against the grain
Chopping roughly.

Today's appointment has finally been
cancelled.
Now strangely uneventful news.
Five days have taught me
Waiting is no formula for instant magic
Crystallised wisdom in a flash
Birthing without embryo forming.
Now, adrenalin's flow has slowed,
Eyes starting less, seeing in the spaces.

Waiting

Mary and Martha-like
Finding life in the slowness uninvited
In the promise only of fresh flowing blood,
Infilling of clean air expelling stale breath,
New-pounding of heart,
Discarding of graveclothes
And glory throbbing tomb-chilled soil, rocks, breezes,
Wounded spirits.
Waiting.

Healing, love-timed and love-basted.

John 11:1-44

Bethel

I would like to think
I could give you
A certain strength,
As you wait
Her death.

But such giving
Is beyond me,
Locked in my heart
Filled with a desire
For your enlivening,
Your healing, new dreaming.

May Another meet your every need
Today,
Bread to eat,
Sustenance for your soul,
And warmth within
For these days of chill winds
And pale, soft light.

And peace be yours:
Enveloping,
Soothing balm
Of the mellow,
Knowing kind,
Fruit of having loved
And wept
Unstintingly.

Genesis 28:20-22
(Australian Hymn Book 49)
'Bethel' – 'house, or place,
of God'

Appendix 1

Index of Scripture passages

Genesis 3, page 27
Genesis 28:20-22, page 154
Genesis 32:31, page 99
Genesis 32, 33, page 113
Exodus 3:1-12, page 10
Exodus 3:1-6, page 11
Exodus 3:1-15, page 13
Exodus 15:22-27, page 119
Exodus 17:1-7, page 36
Exodus 19, page 10
Exodus 32:1-24, page 131
1 Kings 19:1-19, page 139
1 Kings 19:11-13, page 39
1 Kings 19:11, 12, page 48
Psalm 121, page 137
Psalm 139:1-18, page 147
Isaiah 30:20, page 71
Isaiah 50:7, page 33

Matthew 4:1-11, page 29
Matthew 5:3, page 35
Matthew 6:23, page 31
Matthew 14:13, 14, 22-33, page 103
Matthew 14:22-33, pages 45, 118, 119
Matthew 23:37-39, page 80
Matthew 24:36-44, page 92
Matthew 26:6-13, page 81
Matthew 26:14-16, 20-25, page 82
Matthew 26:26-35, page 83
Matthew 26:47-50, page 84
Matthew 26:55-56, page 88
Matthew 26:57-61, page 89
Matthew 27:11-26, page 87
Matthew 28:1-9, page 149
Mark 5:1-20, page 26
Mark 14:32-42, page 85
Mark 14:43-52, page 86
Luke 1:26-38, page 125

Luke 1:39-56, page 122
Luke 2:1-10, page 93
Luke 2:25-32, page 151
Luke 2:41-50, page 123
Luke 4:14-30, page 105
Luke 5:1-11, pages 42, 43
Luke 5:15, 16, page 40
Luke 7:38, page 70
Luke 9:51-62, page 33
Luke 10:39, 41-42, page 49
Luke 12:49, 50, page 19
Luke 18:18-25, page 32
John 2:1-11, page 73
John 6:32, page 53
John 11:1-44, page 153
John 11:1-54, page 41
John 11:33, 38-44, page 100
John 12:27, page 145
John 19:33-37, page 73
Acts 1:16-20, page 82
Acts 17:23, page 48
Romans 15:32, page 59
1 Corinthians 16:17, 18, page 69
Galatians 5:22-23, page 18
Colossians 1:16, 17, page 137
Hebrews 12:14-17, page 36
Hebrews 11:1, page 141
James 3:14-18, page 36

Appendix 2

Barnabas Ministries

The nurturing of Christian spirituality through such means as the development of retreat programs is a key feature of the ministry of Barnabas Ministries Inc., an ecumenical agency designed to meet particular needs of today's Christian leaders. Such programs are developed in consultation with ecclesiastical, para-church, and missionary organisation leaders.

The author, Dr Ross Kingham, became the first Director of Barnabas Ministries in 1986, and initiated programs aimed at the strengthening of the leadership of Australian churches. He has since been joined by a team of consultants who have helped in the development of these programs, which include both preventative and curative strategies.

Preventative strategies, aiming at the sustaining of quality Christian spirituality as a hedge against the destructive effects of burnout, include the devising of creative retreat programs. Such retreats have been held in all Australian States, and in the Australian Capital Territory, generally in denominational retreat settings. Both ordained clergy and lay women and men participate in these retreats. Over two and a half thousand people participated in such retreats in the first nine years in which they have been offered by Barnabas Ministries.

Additionally, retreats are conducted near Canberra, ACT, for individuals, couples and small groups of Christian leaders who are either in crisis, or are seeking discernment regarding particular issues they are facing and concerning which there is a perception that the environment of a retreat would be helpful.

Involved in this ministry with Dr Kingham is a small team of consultants who share in the retreat leadership and counselling.

Further information about Barnabas Ministries Inc. may be obtained from:

The Secretary
Barnabas Ministries Inc.
P.O. Box 57
Duffy ACT 2611
Australia
(06) 295 6766